To Be a
WOLF

A Learning Story
About the Gray Wolf

Carol A. Amato
Illustrated by David Wenzel

BARRON'S

Dedication
To Ms. O'Suji's students who helped...
many thanks.

Text © Copyright 1995 by Carol A. Amato
Illustrations © Copyright 1995 by David Wenzel

All inquiries should be addressed to:
Barron's Educational Series, Inc.
250 Wireless Boulevard
Hauppauge, New York 11788

International Standard Book No. 0-8120-9287-2

Library of Congress Catalog Card No. 95-17155
Library of Congress Cataloging-in-Publication Data

Amato, Carol A.
    To Be a Wolf / Carol A. Amato; illustrated by David Wenzel.
        p. cm.—(Young readers' series)
    ISBN 0-8120-9287-2
    1. Pawnee Indians—Juvenile literature. 2. Wolves—Juvenile literature.
I. Wenzel, David, 1950–   ill. II. Title. III. Series: Amato, Carol A.
Young readers' series.
E99.P3A55 1995
973'.04979—dc20   95-17155
                                                   CIP
                                                   AC

PRINTED IN HONG KONG
5678 9955 987654321

Table of Contents

Chapter 1

Little Wolf Star

Little Wolf Star sat quietly behind a rock. He was hiding from his friends. They would never find him here, he thought. He had run a long way along the river. He took a deep breath. The cool spring air smelled good.

"I will not stay here long," he said to himself.

Just then he heard something moving through the tall grass.

He peeked out from the rock. A furry wolf pup was looking at him! He was black and had a white mark on his chest that looked like a star.

Little Wolf Star stood up and ran home as fast as he could!

"Father, Father!"

Little Wolf Star ran through the open door of the lodge. Chief Wolf Star was fixing his bow. He stopped when he heard his son call.

"What is it, Little Wolf Star?" he asked.

"By the river, by the river! I saw a wolf. A small one. I ran away as fast as I could, before it could eat me!"

Chief Wolf Star laughed. The boy's grandmother and grandfather laughed. Everyone in the lodge laughed.

"We do not mean to laugh at you, Little Wolf Star! You saw a gray wolf pup . . . just a baby. It would not have hurt you. Its den must be nearby."

"But the pup was black, Father, not gray."

"Some gray wolves are black, son. Others are brown and white."

"Then why are they called gray wolves, Father?"

"Because their undercoats of fur are gray," said the Chief.

"Were we wolf pups once, too, Father?"

"Why do you ask?" Chief Wolf Star said.

"Because we are both named Wolf Star."
Everyone laughed again.

"No, we were never wolf pups, but I will tell you about our names.

"We Pawnee are known as the Wolf People. We believe that wolves are special animals. In many ways, we wish to be like them. Our sign for Pawnee is the same as our sign for wolf."

"I think wolves would like to eat us, Father!"

"The wolves will not eat us," said the Chief. "The wolf is a wild animal. It follows the ways of animals who hunt, but we are not food to wolves. It is the buffalo, deer, elk, rabbit, and mouse who should be afraid of the wolf. They are some of the animals it eats.

The Pawnee have learned the ways of the wolf. Wolves are strong and can travel all day. They move across the plains quickly and quietly. They can see two looks away."

"What is two looks away?" asked the boy.

"It means that the wolf can see very far. It can also hear even the smallest sounds."

"When we dress in our wolf-skin robes, we want to become the wolf's spirit . . . to *be* wolf. In these robes, we can sneak up on the enemy camp. They are not surprised to see wolves near their camp. They are very surprised to see that it is the Pawnee who have fooled them."

"Do the wolves think *we* are wolves?" asked Little Wolf Star.

"No one fools the wolves! They are both wise and strong. You will learn, Little Wolf Star, that each wolf has to be wise and strong for the good of its pack. Each Pawnee has to be wise and strong for the good of the tribe. We both defend our land against enemies. Like the wolf, we all need one another to live. We share the wilderness with them and the other animals."

"But why are we named after stars, Father? Do we want to be like stars, too?" asked the boy.

"No, but because the Pawnee honor the wolf, we have named it as a star in the sky. . . the Wolf Star. You and I are honored to have been given the Wolf Star name. In time, you will learn more about Brother Wolf."

Little Wolf Star smiled. He felt proud to be a Pawnee.

The next day, Little Wolf Star said to his Mother and
Father, "I will go look for brother wolf."

"Do not be surprised if you do not find him," said his
mother. "He is very shy."

"Goodby Mother and Father!" Little Wolf Star called
as he ran out of the lodge.

He passed the fields of corn, and walked across the great plain to the river. He brought his small bow and arrow. He tried to hunt jackrabbits, but they were too fast for him. He walked softly, almost without a sound. He tried to see two looks away. He thought he could even hear the clouds passing by.

Little Wolf Star walked for a long time. Then he came to the rock where he had first seen the pup. The pup was not there.

He walked further. Soon he heard yipping and growling nearby. He followed the sounds. He came to a big bush. He stood up and looked over it. The black pup was drinking from a small brook next to the bush.

Four other pups were playing and rolling in the grass nearby. Behind them, Little Wolf Star could see

the large hole of a den. It had been dug out of a sandy bank. Only one wolf was near the den. She was watching the pups while the mother and other pack members were hunting. She looked toward the bush where Little Wolf Star stood, but sensed that he meant no harm.

Suddenly, the black pup walked right over to the bush where the boy was hiding. He looked right into Little Wolf Star's eyes, as he had before. This time, the boy was not afraid. In their looks of trust, he felt the wolf to be his true brother.

The pup returned to his brothers and sisters. They began biting and nipping at one another. The pups were play-fighting, as he did with his own brothers and friends.

"Some day they may really have to fight," thought Little Wolf Star. "For now, they are learning while they play."

Now they all pounced on the adult wolf. She wagged her tail and did not seem to mind. She licked their faces and played with them.

"I will call him White Star," thought the boy.

Suddenly, he heard howling. The other wolves were coming home.

When the pack reached the den site, the pups ran to greet them. They wagged their tails and made happy squeaks. One gray wolf seemed to be watching everything more than the others.

"He must be their leader," thought the boy. This wolf "woofed" softly, then woofed again. He looked toward the rock. The others looked, too, and growled.

They knew he was there! Little Wolf Star shook with
fear. One of the wolves walked closer to him. The wolf
sniffed the air. Then he returned to the others. He made
whining sounds as he walked. For many seconds, none
of them moved. They, too, must have sensed that the
boy was harmless. Little Wolf Star stopped shaking
and watched.

Chapter 4

The Wolf Pack

Until now, the pups had been quiet. Now they began jumping on one of the female wolves.

"She must be the mother," he thought. She was also black, but did not have a white star on her chest. They licked her muzzle. She had brought back food in her stomach. She made the food come back into her mouth for the pups to eat.

"Ugh!" he thought. "I would not want to be a wolf in all ways!"

Another wolf also helped to feed the pups in this way.

Little Wolf Star counted eight adult wolves in the pack family. Many of the wolves helped with the pups. One of them had brought food for the pup-sitter. She ate hungrily.

After the pups had eaten, some of the adult wolves played with them. The adult wolves played with each other, too. One small female had great fun pouncing on others who were sleeping! The boy held his hand over his mouth to keep from laughing out loud.

"They act in many ways like my own family!"
he thought.

He saw that the wolves were friendly toward each
other, too. They licked the father wolf's snout. They let
him know that he was their leader. When they were
near him they kept their tails low and lowered their
bodies. He could see that some of the wolves ranked
higher than others.

The sun began to sink in the sky. The air was quiet and still. One of the wolves began to howl. She lifted her head up to the pink sky. The other wolves joined her. To Little Wolf Star, the sound was both scary and beautiful. He felt a chill go through his body. The sounds carried for miles across the plains. The pups tried to howl, too, but could hardly be heard.

It was late now. He must hurry home. He ran along the river toward the village. Soon he stopped to catch his breath. He raised his head to the sky and howled. Across the dark plains, the wolves howled back.

During that week, the Chief became very sick. The tribe was afraid they would lose their leader. Little Wolf Star was sad but he tried to be brave. He and his brothers and sisters helped at home. There were twenty-five people in the lodge, and there was always work to do. A month passed. There was no time to go to

the wolf den. Every day he looked at his father's wolf-skin robe and remembered the wolves.

Then his father began getting better. While he rested, he told his son many things about gray wolf. Little Wolf Star was so happy when his father was all well again! The boy had also missed the wolves.

In the morning of the next day, Little Wolf Star rolled up his blanket.

"I will pretend this is my wolf-skin robe," he said. He put his blanket across his back.

He left the lodge and ran across the plain along the river. He moved as softly as a wolf. Soon he came to the den site. He hid behind the bush and peeked over it.

The wolves were not there. He walked toward the den and looked into it. Slowly, he crept through the six foot tunnel. It turned right. At the turn was a big, rounded hollow.

"The mother could sleep here," he thought. The burrow then turned upward to another hollow. "And the pups must sleep here. This den is very clean."

Little Wolf Star crawled out of the den and stood up. "They must have moved," he thought. His heart sank. He looked around. He could tell that the wolves had not left long ago. Part of a kill was nearby, and it did not smell much!

"I will find them," he said.

Like a good scout, he followed their tracks. He looked

for other signs, too. He saw fresh markings on the rocks and sand where they sprayed their urine and left their scat or droppings. The boy knew that they did this to mark the territory that they roamed. Their territory could range for many, many miles. He knew he could only travel so far. He must hurry, because it was getting dark.

Little Wolf Star suddenly heard a wolf howl. Then others. He ran as fast as he could toward the sounds.

Soon he came to a grassy stretch of plain near the river's edge. He could see the wolves in the distance, still howling. Near them was a big, dead buffalo. They stopped howling and began eating hungrily. The boy lay

down in the grass by the riverbank and watched them.

Suddenly, the litter of five pups came bounding out of the tall grass not far from him. They ran to the buffalo kill and began eating.

"The pups must now be eating on their own," he thought. "They want to share in the fresh kill." He knew from his father's words that they would not hunt with the others until the fall.

Little Wolf Star saw White Star. In just one month, he had grown much bigger. All of the pups looked more like their parents now. Their tails had grown long and thick, their noses were longer, and their ears stood up straight. After they had all eaten, the wolves lay down to rest and sun themselves.

The boy rested, too. He wondered if the wolves had left the den site for good. Then he remembered the words of his father. Now that the pups were older, they had probably moved to a new resting area. They would stay there two or more months. If this place was not safe, they would move again. Here the pups would learn adult ways.

As he was thinking, Little Wolf Star suddenly heard sounds behind him. He turned to see three white men walking toward him! His father had told him about these men. Many white men had come from far off lands. At first they had been friends with the Indians. Now they wanted to own the Indian's land. They fought. Many white men and Indians were killed. Most of the white men also hated wolves and had killed hundreds of them.

He ran onto the sandy plain. The wolves saw him.
They leaped up and ran toward him.

"Oh, no," the boy cried out. "I'm surrounded!"
But the wolves ran right past him. The alpha wolves
walked close to the men. The other wolves growled and
bared their teeth. The hair on their backs and their
ears stood straight up. They stared deeply into the eyes
of the white men.

At first, the men were so surprised that they could not move. Then they turned and ran away as fast as they could! The wolves watched them run. After a while, they turned and walked away slowly. Little Wolf Star was still shaking. He had never been so afraid in all his life!

Little Wolf Star ran back to the riverbank to get his blanket. He put it over his back. He looked back at the wolves. White Star was looking at him, too. Then he ran as fast as he could toward the village. He stopped to rest. He lifted his head toward the sky and howled. A moment later, a small howl answered him across the moonlit sandy plain.

Afterword

Wolves Yesterday and Today

Wolflike animals lived on earth millions of years ago. They were large, meat-eating animals. They became the wolves we know today. Wolves were once found all over the world in great numbers. They lived in grasslands, swamps, deserts, forests, and mountains.

When the settlers came to North America they killed many wolves. Trappers killed them and sold their skins. Hunters killed them for sport. Many people hated them and killed them for that reason. Thousands of wolves were killed for many years. In time, there were few wolves left in North America, and they became endangered.

Today, the gray wolf is still endangered in 48 states. Because of a law made in 1973, people can no longer kill wolves in North America. In fact, some wolves are now returning from Canada to the central and north-western states on their own. Special groups are trying to protect them as they return. Some of these groups have worked to return wolves to other places in North America where wolves once roamed freely. Wolves were granted freedom into Yellowstone National Park on March 21, 1995. Ranchers are afraid they will attack their cattle and sheep. Wolves seldom do this.

If they do, the groups will pay the ranchers for the loss of the animals.

Many people are still afraid of wolves. They do not know that wolves are shy and keep to themselves. Wolves do not attack people. You may have heard tales about the big, bad wolf. Now you know that these stories are not true.

We now know so much more about why wolves behave as they do. Today, at last, we understand the important part they play in nature. Like people, each animal on earth has a part to play. Wolves were once one of the top predators on land. They helped to keep the balance in nature by killing the prey they were meant to eat.

Today we understand that wolves and people often behave in the same ways. Like the Pawnee and other tribes, many people now honor and respect the wolf's place on earth. To save wolves, people must learn the truth about them.

If we never see a wolf in the wild, we can hope that some of us will hear one howl in the still of a moonlit night.

Glossary

alpha (AL-pha)**:** The alpha male and female are the pack leaders. These two often stay together for life. The alpha wolves help to keep peace in the pack.

bared: Wolves bare their teeth when they want to threaten another animal. To do this, they curl up their lips so that their sharp teeth can be seen.

den: A den is the place where some wild animals such as bears and wolves raise their young. Before wolf pups are born, the mother wolf finds and digs out a safe place for the den. This may be under big tree trunks, in cut banks along rivers or even in caves. Other wolves in the pack often visit the pups in the den, but they do not live there.

earth lodge: The Pawnee Indians lived in villages of houses or lodges. Each village usually had ten to twelve lodges. The lodges were made of logs and covered with earth and grass. Sometimes more than 10 related families lived in one lodge.

gray wolf: There are twenty-seven kinds (subspecies) of gray wolves. Gray wolves once lived all over the world. The gray wolf known as the timber wolf still lives in the forest areas of the world. The gray wolf known as the Arctic wolf lives in the far North and is white. The gray wolf that once lived on the Great Plains in the Midwest (where Little Wolf Star lived) was known as the Great Plains wolf. This wolf is now extinct. Wolves in the same family may be different colors.

Pawnee (PAW-nee): Hundreds of years ago, the Pawnee Indians came from Texas and settled in what is now known as Nebraska. The Pawnee were known as great scouts and brave warriors. They were also a peaceful people. After the settlers took their land, they were forced to live on a reservation. Today, many Pawnees still live on a small reservation in Oklahoma.

ranking: Within the wolf pack, the alpha pair (male and female) are the leaders. They are usually the smartest members of the pack. The other members of the pack usually do what the alpha pair wants them to do. The next ranking wolves are called the *beta* (BE-ta) animals. The youngest animals, such as the pups, are the lowest ranking. The dominance rules of the pack help to keep them from fighting and hurting each other.

resting area: When the wolf pups are about eight weeks old, the pack moves them to one or more new resting areas. These are called *rendezvous sites*. (The first word is pronounced *rahn-de-VOO* and is a French word that means "meeting place.") The rendezvous site is a summer home where the pups learn the ways of adult wolves.

scent markings: To tell other wolves about their territory, wolves spray their urine on tree stumps, rocks, grass, and other things in the wild. They may mark by leaving their droppings (scat, or feces) and scratch the dirt to cover it. Wolves may also mark by rubbing their bodies against things to leave their body scent. Leaving markings is a way of saying, "Stay away. This land is ours!"

sign: There were many languages spoken among the Indian tribes. The tribes often could not understand each other. They decided to make up a sign language by using hand signals that they could all understand.

stare: Wolves stare or look hard at other animals or people to threaten them. A wolf's stare is a strong warning to be careful.

Dear Parents and Educators:

Welcome to the Young Readers' series!

These learning stories have been created to introduce young children to the study of animals.

Children's earliest exposure to reading is usually through fiction. Stories read aloud invite children into the world of words and imagination. If children are read to frequently, this becomes a highly anticipated form of entertainment. Often that same pleasure is felt when children learn to read on their own. Nonfiction books are also read aloud to children but generally when they are older. However, interest in the "real" world emerges early in life, as soon as children develop a sense of wonder about everything around them.

There are a number of excellent read-aloud natural-science books available. Educators and parents agree that children love nonfiction books about animals. Unfortunately, there are very few that can be read *by* young children. One of the goals of the Young Readers' series is to happily fill that gap!

To Be a Wolf is one in a series of learning stories designed to appeal to young readers. In the classroom, the series can be incorporated into literature-based or whole-language programs, and would be especially suitable for science theme teaching units. Within planned units, each book may serve as a springboard to immersion techniques that include hands-on activities, field study trips, and additional research and reading. Many of the books are also concerned with the threatened or endangered status of the species studied and the role even young people can play in the preservation plan.

These books can also serve as read-aloud for young children. Weaving information through a story form lends itself easily to reading aloud. Hopefully, this book and others in the series will provide entertainment and wonder for both young readers and listeners.

C.A.

Guidelines for the Young Reader's Series

In the Classroom

One of the goals of this series is to introduce the young child to factual information related to the species being studied. The science terminology used is relevant to the learning process for the young student. In the classroom, you may want to use multi-modality methods to ensure understanding and word recognition. The following suggestions may be helpful:

1. Refer to the pictures when possible for difficult words and discuss how these words can be used in another context.

2. Encourage the children to use word and sentence contextual clues when approaching unknown words. They should be encouraged to use the glossary since it is an important information adjunct to the story.

3. After the children read the story or individual chapter, you may want to involve them in discussions using a variety of questioning techniques:
   a. Questions requiring *recall* ask the children about past experiences, observations, or feelings. (*Have you ever seen movies or TV programs about wolves?*)
   b. *Process* questions help the children to discover relationships by asking them to compare, classify, infer, or explain. (*Do you have to eat every day? Does the wolf? Why or why not?*)
   c. *Application* questions ask children to use new information in a hypothetical situation by evaluating, imagining, or predicting. (*In what ways would a lateral line help you?*)

At Home

The above aids can be used if your child is reading independently or aloud. Children will also enjoy hearing this story read aloud to them. You may want to use some of the questioning suggestions above. The story may provoke many questions from your child. Stop and answer the questions. Replying with an honest, "I don't know," provides a wonderful opportunity to head for the library to do some research together!

Have a wonderful time in your shared quest of discovery learning!

Carol A. Amato
Language-Learning Specialist

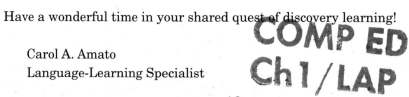